MORE thought PROVOKERS

By Doug Rohrer

Drawings by Joe Spooner

KEY CURRICULUM PRESS
Innovators in Mathematics Education

Copyright © 1994 by Key Curriculum Press. All rights reserved.
Published by Key Curriculum Press, 1150 65th Street, Emeryville, CA 94608.
e-mail: editorial@keypress.com http://www.keypress.com
Graphics by Joe Spooner.

Printed in the United States of America   10 9 8 7   02 01 00   ISBN 1-55953-070-7

Author's Note

This second volume of 50 thought provokers is written with the same intent as the first. Namely, I hope that the reader will find the problems to be intrinsically intriguing and their answers to be counter intuitive. Moreover, the solutions rely more upon creativity and insight rather than formal knowledge or trial and error, though I believe that many of the solutions will illustrate mathematical phenomena. In order to facilitate this learning as well as minimize frustration, a hints section and a solutions section are included as well.

I am indebted to Jeff and Andrea Chow Fanton, Don Helling, Dan and Karen Lane, Catie Stern, and my dad for their suggestions; to Dan Bennett of Key Curriculum Press for his editorial comments; and to Joe Spooner for his illustrations.

—Doug Rohrer

About the Author

Doug Rohrer spent the better part of his formative years in the Washington, D.C. area and later attended the College of William and Mary in Virginia where he majored in Mathematics. In the following five years he taught mathematics at Pinewood School in Los Altos Hills, California, beginning each lecture with the Thought Provoker of the day. He later began mathematical research into memory at the University of California in San Diego, earning his M.A. and Ph.D. in Experimental Psychology. He continues to teach and do research.

The Anchor

While walking along a pier, Annamaria accidentally kicks an anchor into the water but manages to grab onto the end of the rope before it too falls into the water. She then notices that when the rope is pulled taut directly above the anchor, there is 1 foot of rope above the water. If the rope is pulled taut but to the side, the end of the rope touches a point on the water surface 7 feet away from the point on the water surface directly above the anchor.

How deep is the water?

Remember that, in any right triangle, the hypotenuse^2 = leg^2 + leg^2.

Balloon

Jeffrey enjoys driving around town with a helium-filled balloon in his car. The balloon is attached by string to a cupholder between the two front seats so that it "floats" at about the same height as Jeffrey's head. While driving in his hometown one day, the stench of the factories became so great that he had to roll up his windows and close the vents. Suddenly, he was forced to brake the car very quickly. Relative to the cupholder, did the balloon move forward, backward, or not at all? Explain. (You don't need to know anything about helium, except that it is lighter than air.)

The Bank Robbery

As the local sheriff is strolling by the saloon, he hears cries for help from inside the town bank. He rushes inside and sees the bank manager hanging by his waist from a rope tied to the ceiling beam. The banker tells the sheriff that bank robbers tied him up and then took all of the town's money. After looking at the knot in the rope, the sheriff realizes that the banker could not have tied that knot himself without something to stand on. Since there are no desks or ladders near the banker, the sheriff believes him. Later, the sheriff tells the story to his deputy (who is also the town mathematician) and the deputy quickly realizes that the banker is lying. How?

Blocks

Two blocks of wood are each 2 by 2 by 3. Can a hole be cut into one block so that the other block can pass completely through the hole? If yes, how? If not, why not?

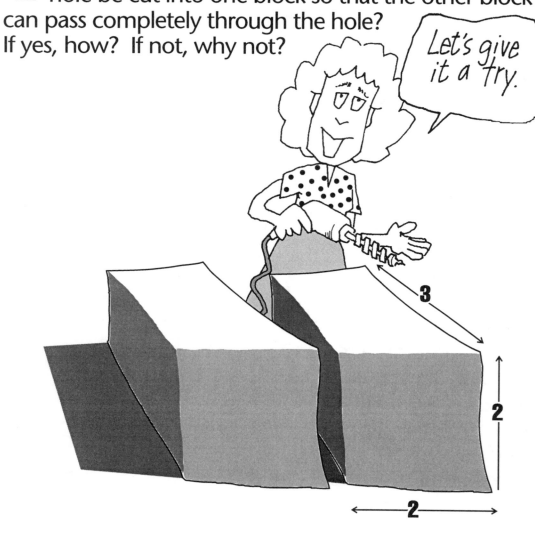

Let's give it a try.

3

2

2

The Canoe

Ryan is canoeing upstream while his sister Katie sleeps in the back of the canoe. As they pass a big tree, one of its branches knocks Katie's hat into the water. Katie wakes up 5 minutes later and discovers that her hat is missing. Ryan instantly turns around and paddles downstream (at the same rate relative to the stream), and they find the hat 1 mile downstream from the big tree. How fast is the stream moving?

The Con Man

Tanya is visiting the big city for the first time. A sinister-looking man asks her is she wants to win some money by guessing the outcome of a sequence of coin flips. Of course, Tanya would never engage in an illegal activity, but she decides that she will first listen to the rules of the game, just out of curiosity, and then encourage the man to seek a better life by using mathematics for good, not evil.

1. Tanya will get the first choice of any sequence of three consecutive coin flip outcomes. Thus, she can choose either HHH, HHT, HTH, HTT, THH, THT, TTH, or TTT.
2. The con man will then get to choose any of the remaining seven sequences.
3. The con man will then toss the coin repeatedly until any three consecutive coin tosses match a sequence chosen by Tanya or the con man. That is, if coin flips 1, 2, 3 do not yield a matching sequence, the coin is flipped again. If coin flips 2, 3, 4 do not yield a matching sequence, the coin is flipped again, and so on, until there is a match.

The con man tells Tanya that she has the advantage since she gets the first choice. Of course, for any choice she makes, the con man will choose the sequence that minimizes Tanya's odds of winning, according to the following table.

Tanya's Choice	HHH	HHT	HTH	HTT	THH	THT	TTH	TTT
Con Man's Choice	THH	THH	HHT	HHT	TTH	TTH	HTT	HTT

How many of Tanya's eight choices give her an advantage? Try to imagine different scenarios and then use your intuition.

The Field of Dreams

Kevin is out in the corn fields one day when he hears a voice say, "If you build it they will come." So Kevin clears out a perfect circle from his crops with an area of one acre. The next day Kevin hears, "No, I want a square," so Kevin forms a square that circumscribes the circle so as to cut down as few crops as possible. On the third day Kevin hears, "Actually, I think I like the circle a little bit better." So Kevin forms a larger circle that circumscribes the square so that the amount of corn cut down is again minimized.

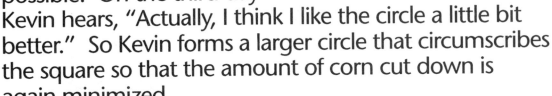

I suppose an octagon is out of the question.

How many acres of corn had Kevin cut down?

Remember that the area of a circle is πr^2 and, for any right triangle, the hypotenuse^2 = leg^2 + leg^2.

The Gold Chain

Camilla is going to an auction tomorrow and she desperately wants that velvet painting of those funny dogs playing cards. At this auction, however, people will bid grams of gold instead of money. She owns a gold chain with 23 links, each weighing 1 gram, and she is willing to spend it all if necessary. But if she wins the painting with a bid of less than 23 grams, she won't be able to give just a portion of the chain, as only a jeweler can cut open a link. Of course, she could have a jeweler cut open every link today, but then any links not spent at the auction would be ruined. So Camilla decides to have the jeweler cut the minimum number of links that still allow her to pay any sum from 1 to 23. For example, she could pay a 13 gram price with a 12 link chain and a single link. After much thought, Camilla figures out a way to do it with just two cuts! How?

Grapefruit

Catie is admiring a spherical grapefruit that is 5 inches in diameter. She cuts 1-inch slices, as shown below. But Catie doesn't like grapefruit, she likes grapefruit skin. Assuming a negligible skin thickness, make an intuitive guess about which slice, if any, has more skin?

Yum!

Grapefruit equator

5 inches

Greek Speak

The 24 letters of the Greek alphabet are listed below, and many look or sound like the letters in the English alphabet. Look at the list for a short while and then try to read the quotations below. You will find each translation easier than the last.

α	alpha	ι	iota	ρ	rho
β	beta	κ	kappa	σ	sigma
γ	gamma	λ	lambda	τ	tau
δ	delta	μ	mu	υ	upsilon
ε	epsilon	ν	nu	φ	phi
ζ	zeta	ξ	xi	χ	chi
η	eta	ο	omicron	ψ	psi
θ	theta	π	pi	ω	omega

ευρεκα!

—Archimedes, 287–212 B.C.

ρεασον ισ ιμμορταλ, αλλ ελσε μορταλ.

—Pythagoras, 582–500 B.C.

θερε αρε ιν φαχτ τωο θινγσ, ψιενσε ανδ οπινιον; θε φορμερ βεγετσ κνοωλεδγε, θε λαττερ ιγνορανχε.

—Hippocrates, 4607–377 B.C.

υνδερ α στονε λυρκσ α πολιτιχιαν.

—Aristophanes, 450–385 B.C.

α γρεατ οξ στανδσ ον μι τονγυε.

—Aeschylus, 525–456 B.C.

The Hexagon of Manhattan

Mrs. Astoria has decided to retire to Miami Beach and give her 8-acre plot of land in downtown Manhattan to her 8 children. However, she tells her children they cannot have the land until they divide it into eight parts equal in shape and size. Unfortunately for the children, the plot of land is in the shape of a perfect hexagon. How can it be done?

Hypocycloids

If a bug sits within the tread of a tire while the tire rolls along the ground, the bug travels along a path known as a cycloid. If the same tire rolls along the inside of a circle, the cycloid becomes a hypocycloid. For example, if the tire's diameter is 1/3 as big as the loop's diameter, the tire rotates three times in one revolution and produces a *deltoid*, meaning "triangle-like." Or, if the tire's diameter is 1/4 as big as the loop's diameter, the tire rotates four times in one revolution and produces an *astroid* (not asteroid), meaning "star-like."

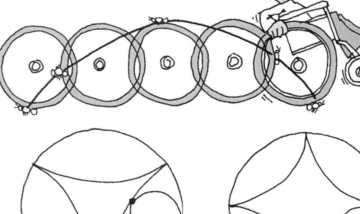
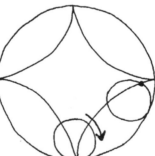

What path is produced if the tire's diameter is 1/2 as big as the loop's diameter?

A deltoid   An astroid

   ©1994 by Key Curriculum Press

Ice Cube

An ice cube is floating in a glass of water so that part of the ice cube is above water level. After the ice cube melts, will the water level in the glass be lower or higher than before, or will it remain the same?

Immortal Turtles

Harry and George aren't your average turtles—they're immortal. Accordingly, they will live forever. They have already done everything a turtle can do, so they decide to spend the rest of their lives walking in a straight line.

Harry decides to travel 1/2 of a mile on the first day, 1/3 of a mile on the second day, 1/4 of a mile on the third day, then 1/5, 1/6, 1/7, and so on.

George decides to travel 1/2 of a mile on the first day, 1/4 of a mile on the second day, 1/8 of a mile on the third day, then 1/16, 1/32, 1/64, and so on.

After an infinite time has passed, how far has each immortal turtle walked?

Hey, George, you want to break for lunch or go on for another century?

Intelligent Life?

Using the most powerful telescope ever made, scientists happened to observe a class of young aliens on a planet millions of light years away. On the blackboard, the teacher had written these equations:

13 + 15 = 31

10 x 10 = 100

6 x 3 = 24

How many fingers did they have?

The Lifeguard

At the lakefront beach, Dan is sitting atop his lifeguard chair and admiring the way he is able to spin a whistle around his finger. Suddenly, a child screams and Dan instantly spots her with his eagle eye, even though she is quite far away. It seems that her raft is losing air quickly and she cannot swim. Dan knows that his running speed in sand is exactly two times his swimming speed. In order to reach this girl as quickly as possible, where along the lake should he enter the water? At *A*, so he swims the shortest distance possible, at *C*, so he travels the shortest total distance possible, or at *B*, the point shown in the figure below between *A* and *C*?

Light Bulbs

There is a very long hallway, longer than the eye can see. Along the midline of its ceiling, there are light bulbs, spaced a few feet apart, for as long as the eye can see. A string hangs from each light bulb; a pull of the string turns the light bulb on, and another pull turns the light bulb off.

A woman begins walking down the hall and pulls every single string, turning all of the light bulbs on. A second woman begins walking down the hall and pulls every second string (2, 4, 6, ...), thereby turning off each of those light bulbs. And then a third woman begins to pull every third string (3, 6, 9, ...), thereby turning some light bulbs on and others off. And then a fourth woman does the same, and then a fifth woman, and so on. Eventually, the women are only pulling strings that are farther away than can be seen. Of those that can be seen, which light bulbs are on?

Manhole Cover Revisited

A previous volume of *Thought Provokers* asked "Why are manhole covers circular?" One answer is that circular manhole covers have a constant diameter. A square manhole cover, for example, could fall diagonally into the hole because a diagonal is longer than a side.

Aren't these ⊙!!⊚ ✿ things supposed to be round?!!

There are, however, shapes besides circles that have constant diameter. Can you visualize such a shape?

Marbles

There are two blue marbles in one cup, two red marbles in a second cup, and a blue and a red marble in a third cup. The three cups are labeled *Blue-Blue*, *Red-Red*, and *Blue-Red*. However, none of these labels correctly describes the marbles in that cup.

By reaching into a cup of your choice and pulling out one marble without looking at the other, how can you determine, without a doubt, the color of the marbles in each cup? Explain your answer.

The Mind Reader

Choose an integer between 2 and 9.
Multiply by 9.
Find the sum of the two digits.
Subtract 3.
Add 1 if your eyes are brown.

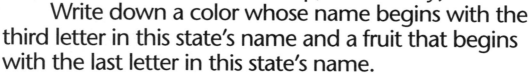

Find the letter in the alphabet that corresponds to this number. For example, 1-A, 2-B, 3-C, 4-D, 5-E, 6-F, 7-G, 8-H, etc.

Think of a U.S. state that begins with this letter (or look at a map, if necessary).

Write down a color whose name begins with the third letter in this state's name and a fruit that begins with the last letter in this state's name.

Now hold this puzzle page upside down in a mirror and read the message below.

Yowza. How did that happen?

There is no such thing as an orange apple.

Mirror on the Wall

Karen is admiring herself in the mirror one day when she notices that the mirror is just long enough to show the entire length of her body. If Karen's height is 66 inches, how long is the mirror?

Not only does the answer not depend upon the distance between her eyes and the top of her head, Karen could take a step forward or backward and the mirror would still show the entire length of her body!

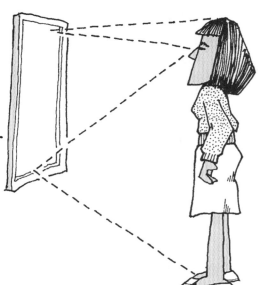

Mixed Nuts

Svetlana had a craving for mixed nuts, but all she had at home was a bag of peanuts and a bag of almonds. So she poured all of the almonds into an empty jar and then poured all of the peanuts on top, which did not quite fill the jar. Svetlana  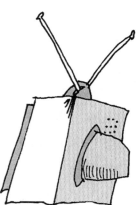 then put on the lid and began to shake the jar up and down while watching educational television. After a few minutes she suddenly realized that the peanuts and almonds were not mixed at all, and the almonds were now on top! In other words, the almonds rose to the top, even though almonds are bigger and heavier than peanuts. In fact, the same thing happens in boxes of cereal and bags of potato chips. Why?

Monkeys in Love

A rope is stretched over a large pulley and there is a monkey on each end of the string. The monkeys are in love, and they wish to express their love by pulling bugs from each other's hair. Unfortunately, they cannot reach each other, so one monkey begins to climb up the rope at 10 feet per minute while the other hangs on tight. Oddly, both monkeys (who weigh the same) begin to rise at the same rate. At what speed do they approach the pulley? Why?

#23

Pay Attention

What is the next letter?

$$W, I, T, N, \_\_$$

©1994 by Key Curriculum Press

The Pizza Paradox

Tom has just made a small pizza pie and a large pizza pie. He cuts a round hole from the center of each and now has two pizza rings. When he places a ruler along side (or tangent to) the hole in each pizza, Tom finds that, for both pizzas, the distance between the outer edges of the pizza is exactly 10 inches. What Tom doesn't realize, however, is that any two pizza rings with 10 inch chords tangent to a hole have the same area (that is, the same amount of pizza). Given that information, what is the area of each pizza ring?

You don't need the size of holes, just remember the area of a circle equals πr^2.

The Pyramid Walk

A couple of Egyptian rats decide that it would be really cool to walk to the top of one of the Great Pyramids. Joe decides to walk directly up the center of one of the sides, whereas Sammy walks along one of the edges. Which path was steeper, or were they equally steep?

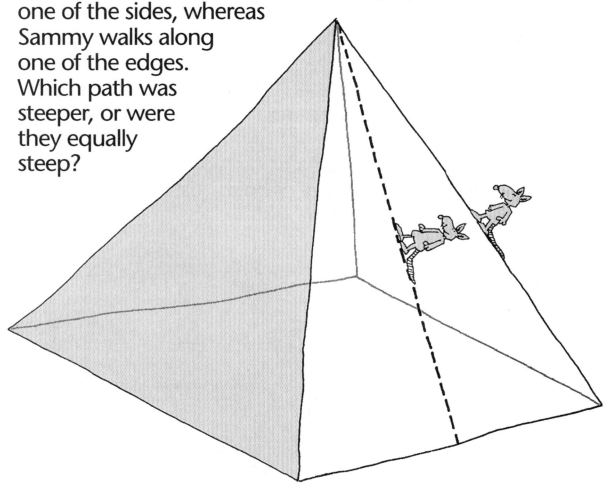

Quadrilaterals

A quadrilateral is any four-sided polygon.

A trapezoid is a four-sided polygon with exactly one pair of parallel sides.

A parallelogram is a four-sided polygon with exactly two pairs of parallel sides.

A rhombus is a parallelogram with four congruent sides.

A rectangle is a parallelogram with four right angles.

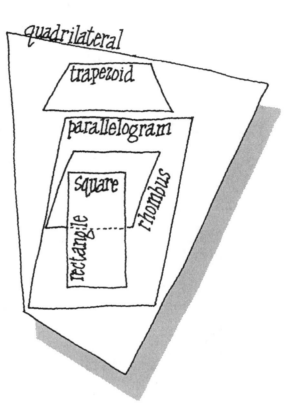

A square is a parallelogram with four congruent sides and four right angles.

These six shapes are shown above (the rhombus and rectangle overlap). Though the figure looks like abstract art, the shapes are actually arranged in a very systematic way. Can you figure it out?

Quesadillas

Nigel's favorite soap opera begins in just 3 minutes, and he is in a panic. He wants to grill 3 quesadillas, 1 minute on each side, but his griddle only holds 2 quesadillas. If he grills 2 quesadillas simultaneously, front and back, and then grills the third quesadilla, front and back, 4 minutes will have elapsed. In other words, he would miss the first minute of his soap opera and would not find out whether Lance, who has amnesia, is actually Giorgio's natural father, or whether Vivian is just having another bad dream. How can he grill the quesadillas in time to watch his soap opera?

Rental Cars

Cross-Country Rent-a-Car only rents cars for five-day and seven-day blocks. For example, one can rent a car for 12 days (5 + 7) or 29 days (3 • 5 + 2 • 7). However, one can NOT rent a car for 18 days, because there is not a multiple of 5 and a multiple of 7 that add to 18.

On a hot summer day a woman walks into the shop and asks if she can rent a car until December 31st, and the salesperson answers "Yes" without any thought at all. When she asks for the price, the salesperson answers, "I'm not sure; what is today's date?"

How did the salesperson know that the number of days until December 31st was a sum of a multiple of 5 and a multiple of 7 without knowing the date? Prove your answer.

The Rice Cooker

Don is camping out by a clear mountain stream and decides to make some rice. The cooking directions ask for 1 quart of water, but Don has only a 7-quart jug and an 11-quart jug. Don hates dry rice and he hates sticky rice. How can he measure out exactly 1 quart?

The Root to Infinity

Solve for x.

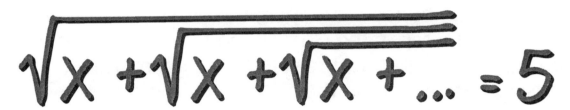

$$\sqrt{x + \sqrt{x + \sqrt{x + \ldots}}} = 5$$

Wow! Infinity's a really long way off!

Rubber Bands

Three rubber bands are interlocked so that none can be separated from the others. However, if any one of the rubber bands is cut open, the other two rubber bands can be separated. That is, no two rubber bands are interlocked, but all three are! For each of the six missing intersections in the diagram below, decide which rubber band passes over the other (the bridge) and which passes underneath (the tunnel).

The Sandboxes

Two sandboxes, one with black sand and one with white sand, each contain the same amount of sand. A child scoops a full bucket of the black sand and pours it into the white sand. The child stirs this mixture for hours until the black and white sand are perfectly mixed. The child then scoops a full bucket of the mixed sand and pours it into the black sand so that both sandboxes once again have the same amount of sand. Which is greater, the amount of black sand added to the white sand or the amount of white sand added to the black sand, or are they equal?

Shuffled Cards

Of the 52 playing cards in a deck, each card has one of 13 values: ace, 2, 3, ... , queen, king. If you were to randomly choose any 2 of these 13 values (e.g., 7 and jack), what are the odds that two cards with these chosen values will be adjacent in a well-shuffled deck? That is, if the cards in the deck were turned face up one at a time, what is the probability that a card with one chosen value will immediately follow a card

with the other chosen value (e.g., a seven of hearts and a jack of clubs in succession)?

Rather than attempt to solve this problem mathematically, give an intuitive estimate of the probability to the nearest five percent.

Siblings

There are three houses next to one another and two kids live in each house. One house has two boys, one house has two girls, and one house has a boy and a girl. If you were to walk into a house at random and see a girl, what is the probability that the other kid in the house is also a girl?

And the answer is not 1/2.

Silver Coins

There are eight silver coins and one counterfeit coin that looks like a silver coin but actually weighs slightly less than the others. By using a balance scale to compare coins (or groups of coins), how can you determine the counterfeit coin with just two weighings?

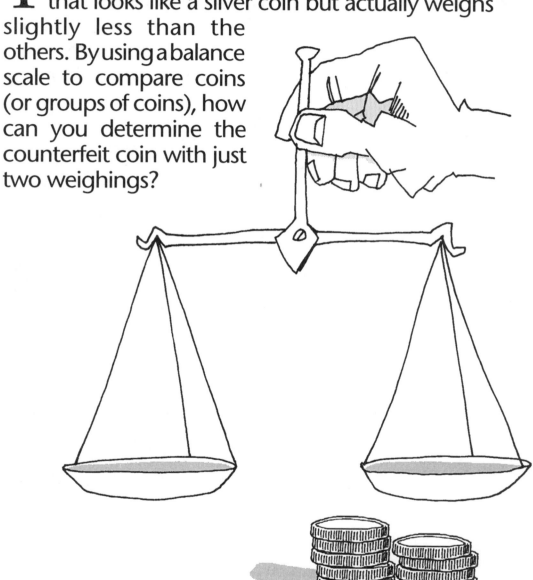

Soapbox Derby

Ariel, Beth, and Carolina, who love to feel the wind in their hair, are each preparing to ride a soapbox derby car down one of two different ramps. Ariel will ride down a ramp with a constant slope while Beth and Carolina will ride down a ramp shaped like one-half of an inverted cycloid, as shown below. (See the Thought Provoker "Hypocycloids" for a description of a cycloid.) Beth will start at the top of the cycloid ramp and Carolina will start about halfway down the ramp. Both ramps cover the same vertical and horizontal distance, though the cycloid ramp is longer than the straight ramp, of course. If all three girls begin at the same time, who will get to the bottom first? Use your intuition.

Spheres

Each of the spheres below has a cylindrical hole 6 cm long drilled directly through it center. Does the smaller sphere have less, more, or the same volume remaining after the hole is drilled? Use your intuition.

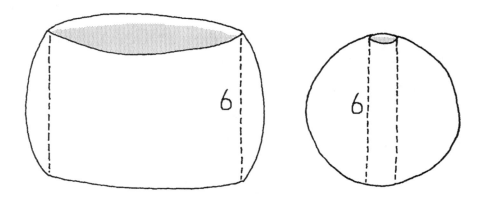

©1994 by Key Curriculum Press

Stairway to the Stars

Suppose that rectangular blocks are stacked on top of each other so that each new block is shifted farther and farther off center, as shown below. Assuming a large enough supply of blocks, how far off center can the top block get before the stack falls down? For example, will the stack fall as soon as the center of the top block is no longer directly above any part of the bottom block? Or will the stack fall as soon as the entire top block is no longer directly above any part of the bottom block?

See if you can intuit the answer. Or try to solve the problem mathematically.

The Surgeon

The town surgeon, whose left arm is in a sling, is in a tizzy. Three of the local men have been struck with appendicitis and each man needs his appendix removed immediately. The surgeon can do the surgery with only her right hand, but there are only two surgical gloves in the doctor's office. If any of the three patients or the doctor makes contact with a nonsterile surface, his or her life will be in danger. How can the doctor perform the surgery?

I should have gone to wall-papering school....

Swim to Alcatraz

Darcy always swims at the same speed. Yesterday she swam from Fisherman's Wharf to Alcatraz Island and back, and there was no current. Today, however, there is a current and she will be swimming directly against the current on the way out and with the current on the way back. Of course, when she swims with (or against) the current, her swimming speed will increase (or decrease) by the speed of the current. Will this swim take more or less time than the swim without the current, or does it not matter?

Tennis Balls in Orbit

If a well-inflated basketball or tennis ball drops to the ground, it will bounce almost as high as the height from which it was dropped.

But suppose you place a tennis ball directly underneath a basketball before simultaneously dropping both from, say, waist high. Will the basketball bounce lower or higher than it would without the tennis ball, or does it not matter?

Or, vice versa, suppose you place a basketball directly underneath a tennis ball before simultaneously dropping both. Will the tennis ball bounce lower or higher than it would without the basketball, or does it not matter?

Think about it first, and then try it. And make sure that both balls are touching as they free fall to the ground. You will be amazed.

WARNING: Wear goggles, do it outside far from other people, and stand behind a pole with your arms wrapped around the pole so that the pole is between your face and your hands.

The Termite

Twenty-seven cube-shaped wood blocks are stacked as one large cube three blocks high, three blocks wide, and three blocks long. A termite is inside the center cube and wishes to burrow a path through all 27 blocks without visiting the same cube twice. The termite can only burrow into an adjacent block that shares a face, not into adjacent blocks that share only an edge or a corner. Can it be done? If so, how? If not, why not?

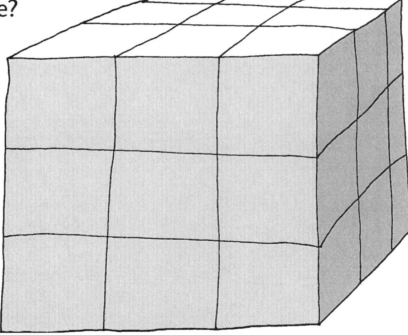

Toothpicks

The 16 toothpicks below form 5 squares. Move just 3 toothpicks so that the 16 toothpicks form 4 squares, all of which are congruent to the original 5 squares. Unlike most problems of this sort, intuition is the best way to solve this problem.

Topography

Topographical maps contain contour lines that connect points of equal elevations, as shown in Figure A. For example, all points between the 1000 and 1500 feet contour lines have elevations between 1000 and 1500 feet. (Likewise, weather maps include lines connecting points with equal temperature.)

In Figure B, the elevations of many points are included, but the contour lines are not. How many mountains are there?

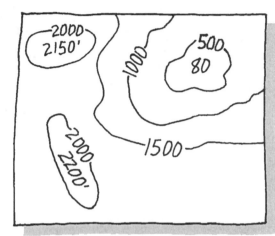

Figure A

Mountains?

1810	1850	1900	1700		1800
		2200			
2300		3000	3050	2800 2100	
2700		2700			
2750 3200	3400			2200	1600
2400 2700		2100	2670		
2350	2200	1650 2150		1900
			2200		
1200	1450				
680	820 1700	2300	1850	1100
38 490	1300 1800			
940	↓	2100 1700 1200	890
1100				

Figure B

The Tray of Glasses

In the tray shown below, holes A, D, E, and F hold glasses filled with water; holes G and H hold empty glasses; and holes B and C are empty. If the tray were lifted with one hand placed directly underneath the center, the tray would not balance. By touching only one glass, alter the configuration of glasses so the tray balances about its center.

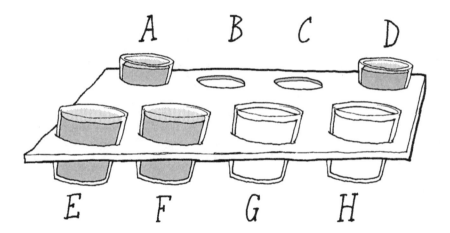

©1994 by Key Curriculum Press

Triangular Numbers

If the square numbers are 1, 4, 9, 16, 25, 36, ... , n^2, what are the *triangular* numbers?

$1, 4, 9, 16, 25, 36, ..., n^2$

Virus

There is a deadly virus in one of the eight liquid samples in your laboratory, but you have forgotten which one it is! There are test kits that can determine the presence of the virus in just a drop of the liquid sample, but you only have three such kits in the lab. Assuming the virus spreads throughout any liquid sample that contains it, how can you locate which sample has the virus?

hmm...

A Walk in the Park

Angela, her dog, and her flightless bird are sitting in the park. Unbeknownst to them, there is a cat sleeping in the park. Coincidentally, the four of them are sitting at the vertices of a square 100 meters on a side (see below). When the cat awakes and stands up, Angela begins running directly toward her dog before it can get the cat. At the same instant, the dog begins running directly toward the cat, the cat begins running directly toward the bird, and the bird begins running directly toward Angela for safety. Yikes! Since each of them is running directly at a moving target, their paths are curved.

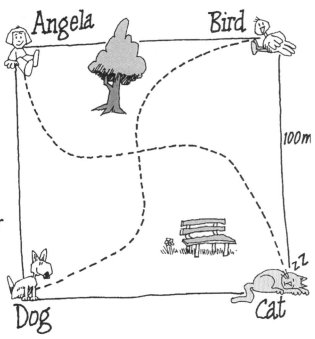

Fortunately, all four of them, who run at the exact same speed, reach the center of the square at the same time, and Angela is able to grab her dog and bird before anybody gets hurt.

How far did each run?

Wax and Tacks

With only a dozen or so thumbtacks and a box of matches, how can you mount two candles onto a wall and light them?

Note: An experimental psychologist presented this problem to college students, one student at a time, and told one half of the students that they would receive twenty dollars for a correct solution. On average, the students who had a chance to win money did worse than those who had no chance to win money.

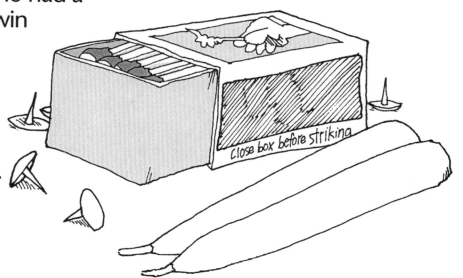

Close box before striking

HINTS

The Anchor

Hint: Solve for x.

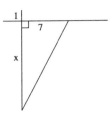

Balloon

Hint: Outside of a car, a helium balloon rises up because air pressure closer to the ground is greater than air pressure higher up. The helium, which is lighter than air, is pushed in the direction of the lesser air pressure. Imagine that all of the air molecules inside the car (but outside the balloon) are little passengers who are not wearing seat belts.

The Bank Robbery

Hint: It turns out that there was a pool of water on the floor beneath the tied-up banker.

Blocks

Hint:

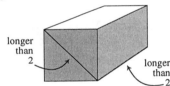

The Canoe

Hint: Note that the time it takes to canoe back to the hat after turning around (the downstream direction) does *not* depend on the rate of the stream. Try to deduce the time needed for the return trip.

The Con Man

Hint: Regardless of what Tanya and the con man choose, both have a 1 in 8 chance of winning after just 3 tosses. But consider what will happen if more coin flips are needed.

The Field of Dreams

Hint: Let the radius of the smaller circle equal r and try to find the length of the hypotenuse of the right triangle shown .

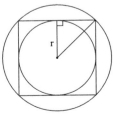

The Gold Chain

Hint: If just one middle link is cut, the chain is divided into *three* pieces, not just two.

Grapefruit

Hint: What happens to the circumference of rings as you go from the pole to the equator? What happens to the width of the rings?

Greek Speak

Hint: The first phrase translates to "Eureka!"

The Hexagon of Manhattan

Hint: Think trapezoids.

Hypocycloids

Hint: Where is the bug after the tire has rolled 1/4 of the way around the loop?

Ice Cube

Hint: When an ice cube floats on the surface, it weighs as much as the water it displaces. That is, if half of the ice cube is under water, then the water that could fill that submerged space weighs as much as the entire ice cube.

Immortal Turtles

Hint: For each turtle, find the sum of the first two walks, then the sum of the first three walks, the sum of the first four walks, and so on. By observing the way in which these sums increase, you can intuit the sum of all of the walks for each turtle.

Intelligent Life?

Hint: The symbol "11" represents $10 + 1$, where "10" represents the number of fingers.

The Lifeguard

Hint: Think about what you gain or lose entering the water just a little to either side of point A or C.

Light Bulbs

Hint: For any particular light bulb position, the number of its factors equals the number of string pulls. For example, since 6 has 4 factors (1, 2, 3, and 6), the sixth light bulb will be pulled four times (on, off, on, off).

HINTS

Manhole Cover Revisited

Hint: Start with an acute triangle with extended sides. Use a compass and swing arcs from the corners of the triangle to create a shape with constant diameter.

Marbles

Hint: Which cup must have two marbles of the same color?

The Mind Reader

Hint: For any multiple of 9 with two digits (18, 27, 36, 45, 54, 63, 72, 81) the digits always add to 9.

Mirror on the Wall

Hint: Label the distance between the top of her head and her eyes as x and the distance from her eyes to the floor as y. Now try to find the length of the mirror portions above and below eye level.

Mixed Nuts

Hint: Each time the jar is shaken up and down, the nuts rise and leave small gaps between all the nuts.

Monkeys in Love

Hint: The amount of the rope between the two monkeys is decreasing at 10 feet per minute.

Pay Attention

Hint: Read the question again.

The Pizza Paradox

Hint: You're told in the problem that the answer does not depend on the diameter of the hole. You can get an intuitive sense of why this is true by recognizing that a very large pizza would have a large diameter hole in order to maintain a 10-inch tangent chord. The ring would have a large circumference, but not much width. If you decrease the circumference, the width of the ring increases, leaving a constant area of pizza. Given that fact, try a hole diameter that makes it easy to find the area of the pizza ring.

The Pyramid Walk

Hint: Consider how far each rat walked.

Quadrilaterals

Hint: All trapezoids are quadrilaterals, but not all quadrilaterals are trapezoids.

Quesadillas

Hint: One of the quesadillas is grilled on one side, then removed, then grilled on the other side.

Rental Cars

Hint: One can rent a car for 24, 25, 26, 27, or 28 days.

The Rice Cooker

Hint: Remember that water can be poured back into the stream.

The Root to Infinity

Hint: Square both sides, but only *once*. Then look for a clever substitution.

Rubber Bands

Hint: If an ant were to crawl along any one of the rubber bands, it would never encounter two "bridges" or two "tunnels" in a row. That is, no two consecutive intersections are both bridges or both tunnels.

The Sandboxes

Hint: Though the answer does not depend on the amount of sand in the sandbox or the size of the bucket, it may be easier to assign arbitrary values to these quantities. For example, suppose that each sandbox originally contained 9 gallons of sand and the bucket holds 1 gallon of sand.

Shuffled Cards

Hint: Try it. But make sure that you shuffle the cards seven or eight times between each trial.

Siblings

Hint: The probability of an event equals the number of possible outcomes in which the event occurs divided by the total number of *equiprobable* possible outcomes.

Silver Coins

Hint: First compare coins 1-2-3 and coins 4-5-6.

HINTS

Soapbox Derby

Hint: Even though Beth must travel farther than Ariel (the shortest distance between two points is a straight line), Beth gains speed more rapidly at first, as the cycloid ramp is initially very steep.

Spheres

Hint: Imagine two other examples which are much more extreme so that any difference, if one exists, will be magnified.

Stairway to the Stars

Hint: Consider the right edge of each block as a fulcrum underneath a teeter-totter that holds the blocks above it.

The Surgeon

Hint: There are four people and four glove surfaces, allowing each person his or her own surface.

Swim to Alcatraz

Hint: Though the answer is independent of the speed of the swimmer and current, you may want to assign values to these unknowns. For example, let Darcy swim 4 miles per hour, the current be 1 mile per hour, and the island be 1 mile away. These values yield a "clean" solution that doesn't require a calculator.

Tennis Balls in Orbit

Hint: Just do it. In one case, the bottom ball acts like a shock absorber. In the other case, the bottom ball acts like a trampoline. Which ball do you think would act like a trampoline? What would that do to the other ball?

The Termite

Hint: Imagine that the 1 center block and the 12 blocks in the center of each edge of the large cube are painted blue and the 14 remaining blocks are painted white. Therefore, any two blocks that have a face in common are different colors.

Toothpicks

Hint: Because 4 squares, with 4 sides each, use up all 16 toothpicks, the 4 squares must not have any sides in common.

Topography

Hint: Roughly sketch the contour lines for 500, 1000, 1500, 2000, 2500, and 3000 feet, beginning with the higher elevations. Make sure that all the points between any two adjacent lines include only the appropriate elevations.

The Tray of Glasses

Hint: Four of the glasses are filled with *water*.

Triangular Numbers

Hint: $1, 4, 9, 16, ... , n^2$ pebbles can be arranged in a square array.

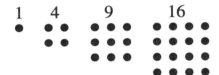

Virus

Hint: By mixing a small sample from several bottles into a new bottle, you can determine whether the virus is or is not in one of those bottles.

A Walk in the Park

Hint: Since each creature is running directly at its target, the paths of the chaser and its chasee are always at right angles.

Wax and Tacks

Hint: Beware of *functional fixedness*, the inclination to forget that an object can be used for purposes other than those for which it was designed.

ANSWERS

The Anchor

Answer:

$$(x + 1)^2 = x^2 + 7^2$$
$$x^2 + 2x + 1 = x^2 + 49$$
$$2x + 1 = 49$$
$$x = 24$$

Balloon

Answer: Backwards.

When the car brakes suddenly, the air molecules inside the car (but outside the balloon) rush forward, just like human passengers. Then the air towards the front of the passenger cab becomes very dense with tightly packed air molecules whereas the air molecules behind the balloon are packed much more loosely. This air pressure in the front of the car pushes backwards with enough force to move things lighter than the air (the helium balloon) but not with enough force to change the direction of things heavier than air (like human passengers). So the balloon is pushed backward, but human passengers lunge forward.

The Bank Robbery

Answer: The banker stood on a large block of ice while tying himself up and then waited for the ice to melt before crying for help.

Blocks

Answer:

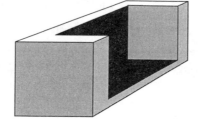

The Canoe

Answer: Note that the time it takes to canoe back to the hat after turning around (downstream) does *not* depend on the rate of the stream. Think of the stream as a giant conveyor belt where a 5 minute walk away from the hat requires a 5 minute walk back to the hat. Therefore, the 1 mile trip of the hat took 10 minutes, which is 6 miles per hour.

The Con Man

Answer: None of them.

Even though Tanya and the con man have a 1/8 chance of correctly guessing three coin tosses in a row—(1/2)(1/2)(1/2) = 1/8—the con man's choice increases his chance of victory if the game lasts longer than three tosses. Notice that his second and third choices are always Tanya's first two choices, but his first two choices are never Tanya's second and third choices. This gives him more opportunities to win before she can.

The Field of Dreams

Answer: Two acres.

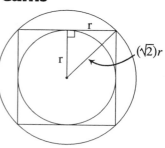

If the radius of the smaller circle equals r, then the smaller circle has an area of $\pi r^2 = 1$ acre. The hypotenuse of the right triangle shown at right has a length of $(\sqrt{2})r$. Therefore, the area of the larger circle equals $2\pi r^2$, or $2 \cdot 1$ acre.

The Gold Chain

Answer: By cutting open the fourth and the eleventh link, obtaining links of lengths 3, 1, 6, 1, and 12, any sum between 1 and 23 is possible.

1	12 + 1
1 + 1	12 + 1 + 1
3	12 + 3
3 + 1	12 + 3 + 1
3 + 1 + 1	12 + 3 + 1 + 1
6	12 + 6
6 + 1	12 + 6 + 1
6 + 1 + 1	12 + 6 + 1 + 1
6 + 3	12 + 6 + 3
6 + 3 + 1	12 + 6 + 3 + 1
6 + 3 + 1 + 1	12 + 6 + 3 + 1 + 1
12	

ANSWERS

Grapefruit

Answer: Each slice has the same amount of skin. The slice at the pole has less circumference, but it has skin going all the way to the center. As you move towards the equator, the circumference becomes greater, but the rings of skin decrease in width. These two factors balance each other out and leave a constant area of skin.

Greek Speak

Answers:

Eureka!

Reason is immortal, all else mortal.

There are in fact two things, science and opinion; the former begets knowledge, the latter ignorance.

Under each stone lurks a politician.

A great ox stands on my tongue.

The Hexagon of Manhattan

Answer:

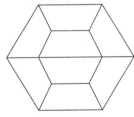

Hypocycloids

Answer: A straight line.

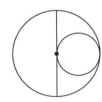

Ice Cube

Answer: The water level doesn't change. When an ice cube floats on the surface, it weighs as much as the water it displaces. That is, if half of the ice cube is under water, then the water that could fill that displaced space weighs as much as the entire ice cube. And that amount of water must be the same amount of water that is in the ice cube because an ice cube weighs the same frozen as it does unfrozen. (Before melting, the ice cube is less dense and greater in volume.)

Immortal Turtles

Answer: Harry walked an infinite distance and George walked only 1 mile.

Consider how far Harry and George have walked after each of the first four days:

	Day 1	Day 2	Day 3	Day4
Harry	$\frac{1}{2}$	$\frac{1}{2}+\frac{1}{3}=\frac{5}{6}$	$\frac{5}{6}+\frac{1}{4}=\frac{13}{12}$	$\frac{13}{12}+\frac{1}{5}=\frac{77}{60}$
George	$\frac{1}{2}$	$\frac{1}{2}+\frac{1}{4}=\frac{3}{4}$	$\frac{3}{4}+\frac{1}{8}=\frac{7}{8}$	$\frac{7}{8}+\frac{1}{16}=\frac{15}{16}$

While Harry walks less far each day than the day before, his total distance at the end of each day is a fraction whose numerator is increasing faster than the denominator. The total distance he walks can increase indefinitely. The total distance George walks approaches 1 mile. In fact, each day he covers only 1/2 the distance remaining between him and the 1 mile mark.

Harry's walk was a **harmonic sequence**. In such a sequence, the reciprocals of each term (the reciprocals of 1/2, 1/3, 1/4, ... are 2, 3, 4, ...) increase by the same amount. In this case, the constant increase of the reciprocals is 1. George's walk was a **geometric sequence**. In that kind of sequence, each number, when multiplied by some constant (in this case 1/2), gives the next number. For example, (1/2)(1/2) = 1/4, and (1/4)(1/2) = 1/8, and (1/8)(1/2) = 1/16.

Intelligent Life?

Answer: Seven. That is, they counted in base 7: 1, 2, 3, 4, 5, 6, 10, 11, 12, 13, 14, 15, 16, 20, 21, 22, 23, ...

Written in base 10, the alien equations are:

$(7 + 3) + (7 + 5) = (3 \cdot 7) + 1$

$7 \cdot 7 = 49$

$6 \cdot 3 = (2 \cdot 7) + 4$

The Lifeguard

Answer: There's a particular point B between A and C that minimizes the total travel time.

Entering the water just left of point A wouldn't make sense because Dan would increase both his running distance and his swimming distance. But if he enters just to the right of point A, he can cut off a running distance that is more than twice the swimming distance he'd add to the trip.

Entering at point *C* would make sense if he could swim as fast he can run, but because he can run faster, it makes sense to enter to the left of *C*, running a little farther but shortening his swim.

So the optimal entry point is between *A* and *C*. It turns out that this optimal point *B* is the point where the ratio of *BD* to the distance run is twice the ratio of *AB* to the distance swum (because the running speed is twice the swimming speed).

This problem is analagous to that of light passing from one medium to another (e.g., from air to water). For example, when you stand at the side of a pool and look at an object inside the pool, the path of light from the underwater object to your eye bends at the surface of the water, which is why the object appears to be in the wrong place.

Light Bulbs

Answer: 1, 4, 9, 16, 25, ... , n^2.

For any particular light bulb position, the number of its factors equals the number of times its string was pulled. For example, since 6 has 4 factors (1, 2, 3, and 6), the sixth light bulb string will be pulled 4 times (on, off, on, off). If a light bulb position has an even number of factors, then the light bulb will be off (on, off, ... , on, off), but if a light bulb position has an odd number of factors, the light bulb will be on (eg., on, off, ... , on, off, on). Factors usually come in pairs, and a light bulb position with an odd number of factors must be a square. For example, 9 (1, 3, and 9) and 16 (1, 2, 4, 8, and 16) both have an odd number of factors.

Manhole Cover Revisited

Answer: Start with your compass point at point *B* and draw an arc *DE* as shown in the illustration in the next column. Move the compass point to point *A* and draw arc *EF*. From *C* draw arc *FG*. From *B* draw arc *GH*. From *A* draw arc *HJ*, and from *C* draw arc *JD*.

All the small arcs have the same radius, as do all the large arcs. So all segments drawn across the figure through any vertex have the same length.

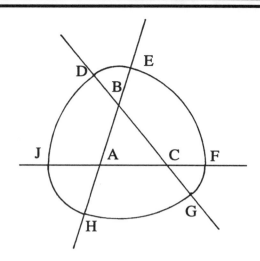

Marbles

Answer: Pull a marble from the Blue-Red cup. If this marble is blue, then the other marble in that cup must be blue. Therefore, two red marbles, which cannot be inside the Red-Red cup, must be inside the Blue-Blue cup. That means the Red-Red cup must contain one blue marble and red marble.

If instead the chosen marble is red, then the other marble in that cup must be red. Therefore, two blue marbles, which cannot be inside the Blue-Blue cup, must be inside the Red-Red cup. That means the Blue-Blue cup must contain one blue marble and red marble.

The Mind Reader

Answer: For any multiple of 9 that has two digits (18, 27, 36, 45, 54, 63, 72, 81), the digits always add to 9. Therefore, one will always search for a state that begins with "F" or "G", depending upon one's eye color. Florida and Georgia are the only two such states, and both states have the same third and last letters.

Mirror on the Wall

Answer: 33 inches.

When Karen looks at herself in a mirror, the mirror is halfway between her and where she sees her mirror image. So her line of sight from her eye to the mirror image of her foot passes through a point on the mirror that is halfway between her eye

ANSWERS

and her foot. Likewise, the line of sight from her eye to the mirror image of the top of her head passes through a point on the mirror that is halfway between her eye and the top of her head. The sum of the portions of the mirror below and above eye level is $(1/2)x + (1/2)y = (1/2)(x + y) = (1/2)(66$ inches$) = 33$ inches. So a "full length" mirror need only be half length!

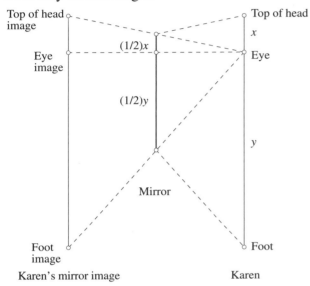

Karen's mirror image   Karen

Mixed Nuts

Answer: The nuts rise into the air each time the jar is shaken up and down, leaving small gaps between all the nuts. Many of these gaps are too small for almonds to squeeze through, but not too small for the peanuts. Eventually, all of the peanuts reach the bottom.

Monkeys in Love

Answer: 5 feet per minute.

Pay Attention

Answer: L.
"**W**hat **I**s **T**he **N**ext **L**etter?"

The Pizza Paradox

Answer: Even if the hole had diameter zero, the area of the pizza ring would remain unchanged. If a pizza ring has no hole, the 10 inch tangent is the diameter of the circle and the pizza has area 25π square inches. Any pizza with a 10 inch chord tangent to a hole has area 25π square inches.

The Pyramid Walk

Answer: Joe's path was steeper. Joe's walk up the center was shorter than Sammy's walk up the edge but both rats climbed to the same height. Therefore, Sammy's longer walk rose more gradually than Joe's.

Quadrilaterals

Answer: The figure is a Venn Diagram. Since a quadrilateral cannot be both a trapezoid and a parallelogram, those two shapes do not overlap. Since a rhombus, rectangle, and square are always parallelograms, these shapes are inside the parallelogram. Since a square is both a rhombus and a rectangle, the square represents the overlap of the rhombus and rectangle. Finally, all of these shapes, which are all quadrilaterals, are inside the quadrilateral.

Quesadillas

Answer: Let quesadillas 1, 2, and 3 have sides A and B. First grill 1A and 2A for one minute. Then grill 2B and 3A for one minute. Finally, grill 1B and 3B for 1 minute.

Rental Cars

Answer: 23 is the greatest number of days that one *cannot* rent a car.

Proof: Note that one can rent a car for 24, 25, 26, 27, or 28 days because
$$24 = 2 \cdot 5 + 2 \cdot 7$$
$$25 = 5 \cdot 5$$
$$26 = 5 + 3 \cdot 7$$
$$27 = 4 \cdot 5 + 7$$
$$28 = 4 \cdot 7$$
Therefore, since one can always rent a car for an extra 5 days, one can also rent a car for
$$24 + 5 = 29 \text{ days}$$
$$25 + 5 = 30 \text{ days}$$
$$26 + 5 = 31 \text{ days}$$
$$27 + 5 = 32 \text{ days}$$
$$28 + 5 = 33 \text{ days}$$
Likewise, one can rent a car for another 5 days, and so on. Therefore, one can rent a car for any number of days greater than 23.

ANSWERS

The Rice Cooker

Answer: Here are the steps.

	7-quart jug	11-quart jug
Fill 11	0	11
Empty 11 into 7	7	4
Empty 7 into stream	0	4
Empty 11 into 7	4	0
Fill 11	4	11
Empty 11 into 7	7	8
Empty 7 into stream	0	8
Empty 11 into 7	7	1

The Root to Infinity

Answer: After squaring both sides, one obtains

$$x + \sqrt{x + \sqrt{x + \sqrt{x + \ldots}}} = 25$$

Since the nasty second term on the left side of this equation is identical to the left side of the original equation, this term must equal 5. Therefore, $x + 5 = 25$, and $x = 20$.

Rubber Bands

Answer:

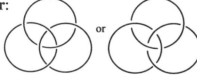

The Sandboxes

Answer: Equal.

The answer does not depend on the amount of sand in the sandbox or the size of the bucket, but we will assume, for simplicity, that each sandbox originally contained 9 gallons of sand and the bucket holds 1 gallon of sand. After the bucket of black sand is added to the white sand, that mixed pile is 1/10 black. When the bucket is filled with mixed sand, it contains 1/10 gallon black and 9/10 gallon white, leaving 9/10 gallon black sand in the white sand pile. And after a bucket of mixed sand is poured into the black sand pile, that pile contains 9/10 gallon of white sand.

Shuffled Cards

Answer: Almost 50%!

Siblings

Answer: There are 3 girls and each is equally likely to be the girl you have seen. Since 2 of these 3 live in a house with another girl, there is a 2/3 chance that the other kid in the house is also a girl.

Silver Coins

Answer: Compare 1-2-3 and 4-5-6.
    If 1-2-3 < 4-5-6, compare 1 and 3.
        If 1 < 3, 1 is counterfeit.
        If 1 = 3, 2 is counterfeit.
        If 1 > 3, 3 is counterfeit.
    If 1-2-3 = 4-5-6, compare 7 and 9.
        If 7 < 9, 7 is counterfeit.
        If 7 = 9, 8 is counterfeit.
        If 8 > 9, 9 is counterfeit.
    If 1-2-3 > 4-5-6, compare 4 and 6.
        If 4 < 6, 4 is counterfeit.
        If 4 = 6, 5 is counterfeit.
        If 4 > 6, 6 is counterfeit.

Soapbox Derby

Answer: Beth and Carolina will reach the bottom first in a tie, even though Beth rode farther than Ariel! Beth gains speed quite rapidly at first, as the cycloid ramp is initially very steep, and her speed continues to increase even as her ramp begins to flatten out. In fact, given a height and a horizontal distance to travel, the cycloid shape provides a quicker descent than any other shape.

In 1696, Johann Bernoulli posed this *brachistochrone problem* (from the Greek for "shortest time") to other mathematicians and it was solved by Newton, Leibniz, L'Hôpital, and Johann's brother Jacob Bernoulli.

Regardless of where Carol begins, Beth and Carol finish at the same time, even though Beth travels farther! Again, Beth's initial vertical descent is steeper than Carol's, allowing her to accelerate faster and catch up at the bottom. The unique properties of the cycloid dictate a perfect tie, solving the *tautochrone problem* (from the Greek for "same time").

ANSWERS

Spheres

Answer: The same. In fact, if the diameter of the hole shrank to nothing, a sphere with diameter 6 cm results, and the volume of that sphere, 36π cm^3, equals the volume remaining in each of the drilled spheres.

Stairway to the Stars

Answer: Theoretically, there is no limit! In practice, static friction and air pressure may keep you from reaching infinity, but it is still relatively easy to stack the blocks so that no portion of the top block is directly above the bottom block.

Mathematically, the shifted distance of each block in the stack, beginning with the top block, grows as a harmonic sequence, $1/2 + 1/3 + 1/4 + 1/5 + 1/6 + ... + 1/n$, which equals infinity.

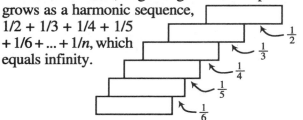

The Surgeon

Answer: Let gloves 1 and 2 have surfaces A and B. For the first surgery, the surgeon uses both gloves on her one good hand, with glove surface 1A touching her hand and glove surface 2B touching patient 1. For the second surgery, the surgeon removes glove 2 so that glove surface 1B touches patient 2. For the third surgery, the doctor turns glove 2 inside out and places it over glove 1 so that glove surface 2A touches patient 3.

Swim to Alcatraz

Answer: More time.

Though the increase in her swimming speed is one direction equals the decrease in her swimming speed in the other direction, the time elapsed during each direction does not change by the same amount. For example, suppose that Darcy swims 4 miles per hour, the current is 1 mile per hour, and the island is 1 mile away. Without the current, at 4 miles per hour, the swim requires 15 minutes each way, for a total of 30 minutes. With the current, at 5 miles per hour, the swim requires $60/5 = 12$ minutes in one direction and $60/3 = 20$ minutes in the other, for a total of 32 minutes. The faster the current, the slower the total swim.

Tennis Balls in Orbit

Answer: If the tennis ball is underneath the basketball, the basketball bounces less high than it would by itself. The tennis ball acts like a shock absorber. If the tennis ball is on top, the tennis ball bounces much higher than usual. The basketball acts like a trampoline. In one of the classes taught by this author, we were able to affix a paper cylinder that allowed us to place two tennis balls atop the basketball. We dropped them from 8 or 10 feet high. Watch for low flying aircraft!

The Termite

Answer: No.

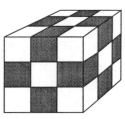

Imagine that the 1 center block and the 12 blocks in the center of each edge of the large cube are painted blue and the 14 remaining blocks are painted white so that any 2 blocks that have a face in common are different colors. Therefore, the termite must always burrow from a blue to a white block or from a white to a blue block. Since the termite burrows through blocks of alternating colors and begins in a blue block, it cannot visit more white blocks than blue blocks. But there are more white blocks than blue blocks comprising the large cube, so it cannot be done.

Toothpicks

Answer:

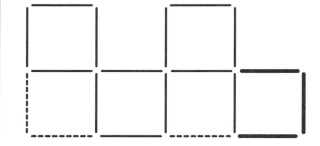

ANSWERS

Topography

Answer: Three mountains (and one basin).

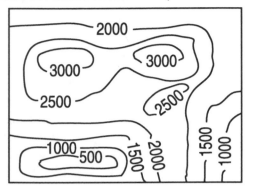

The Tray of Glasses

Answer: Pick up the filled glass in hole F, pour it into the empty glass in hole H, and then place the now empty glass into hole B.

Triangular Numbers

Answer: 1, 3, 6, 10, 15, 21.... The nth triangular number would be $n + (n - 1) + (n - 2) + ... + 1$, or $n(n + 1)/2$.

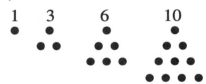

Triangular numbers arise often in mathematical problems. For example, the number of possible handshakes in a group of people is triangular: 2 people, 1 handshake; 3 people, 3 handshakes; 4 people, 10 handshakes. As an added challenge, try to find the sequence of pentagonal or hexagonal numbers.

Virus

Answer: First mix a small sample from four bottles into a new bottle and test that sample. If this sample tests negative (not there), remove these four bottles. If the sample tests positive, remove the other four bottles.

Of the remaining four bottles, mix a small sample from two of them into another new bottle and test that sample. If negative, remove these two bottles. If positive, remove the other two bottles.

Of the remaining two bottles, test either one. If negative, the other bottle contains the virus. If positive, that bottle contains the virus.

Notice that 8 samples require 3 test kits because $2^3 = 8$. If there were 128 samples, 7 test kits would be required because $2^7 = 128$.

A Walk in the Park

Answer: 100 meters.

Since each creature is running directly at its target, the paths of the chaser and its chasee are always at right angles. That is, the distance between the chaser and its chasee depends only on the movement of the chaser, not its chasee. Therefore, the distance that the chaser runs is the same as if its chasee did not run at all, or 100 meters.

Wax and Tacks

Answer: Thumbtack the matchbox upside down to the wall.

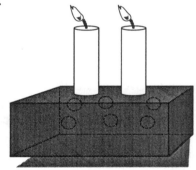